FIELDS OF LIGHT AND STONE

Fields
of
Light
and
Stone

Angeline
Schellenberg

UNIVERSITY
of **ALBERTA**
PRESS

Published by

University of Alberta Press
1-16 Rutherford Library South
11204 89 Avenue NW
Edmonton, Alberta, Canada T6G 2J4
uap.ualberta.ca

Library and Archives Canada Cataloguing in Publication

Title: Fields of light and stone / Angeline Schellenberg.
Names: Schellenberg, Angeline, 1973– author.
Series: Robert Kroetsch series.
Description: Series statement: Robert Kroetsch series | Poems.
Identifiers: Canadiana (print) 20190208627 | Canadiana (ebook) 20190208651 |
    ISBN 9781772125115 (softcover) | ISBN 9781772125214 (PDF)
Classification: LCC PS8637.C4323 F54 2020 | DDC C811/.6—dc23

First edition, first printing, 2020.
First printed and bound in Canada by Houghton Boston Printers, Saskatoon,
    Saskatchewan.
Editing by Alice Major.

A volume in the Robert Kroetsch Series.

University of Alberta Press is committed to protecting our natural environment.
As part of our efforts, this book is printed on Enviro Paper: it contains 100% post-
consumer recycled fibres and is acid- and chlorine-free.

University of Alberta Press gratefully acknowledges the support received for its
publishing program from the Government of Canada, the Canada Council for the
Arts, and the Government of Alberta through the Alberta Media Fund.

for all who seek comfort in story

with love for these imperfect saints

Contents

Everything There Is to Say

An earthquake, but the Lord was not in the earthquake...
A fire, but the Lord was not in the fire.
Finally,...a gentle breeze.
—1 Kings 19:11–12

Everything there is to say
has already been said about trees.
My evergreens never slept.
The Siberian elms (like my ancestors)
would not stay in one place;
they sent defiant seeds searching
for a home on distant lawns and
under foundations, resistant
to tugs. And every time
I tore from my wooden house
in tears, ran for the border
between fields—my shelter-
belt—everyone knows
what the aspens
whispered.

IN SOME REMINISCENT HOUR

Abram John Froese
(January 9, 1919–October 20, 1997)

Margaret Dueck Froese
(March 20, 1922–January 31, 2009)

Love Letters, 1944–45

Abe, Ontario   *Margaret, Manitoba*

I really hadn't thought I would be stationed
as far from you as all this.

But distance doesn't diminish
my love for you.

I must let you in on a little secret.

Time in Evergreen

Resurrection

Very truly I tell you, unless a kernel of wheat
falls to the ground and dies, it remains only a single seed.
—*John 12:24*

I looked for my grandpa in his Bible
and found *Abram John.*

I looked for him behind his desk
and found drawers too small to hold
his regrets.

I looked for him in the stars
and found his spectacles, his trimmed
whiskers floating.

I looked for my grandpa
in his handwritten sermons
and found only Madame Guyon and God.

Grandpa's house had a study where I built
blocks into stairways for the angels.

Grandpa's spirit came to me at night
and took me to Burger King.

He said, *I have to go into the ground*
but I've found

God's house has many rooms
warm as a husk.

Dearest Abe,
Do you think you can forget
about your studies just for a
minute tonight?

Tokens of Mercy

The way Grandpa leans through the window of the idling truck
to pray for another farmer, with thanks for God's *tokens of mercy*,
while

I sweat up the dusty seat to CFAM's farm report: barley down,
drunkenness up; across the road, the Busy "B" ice cream stand, its
sweet rewards for

patience miles away, the way he pulls coveralls over suit and tie,
so he can go from harvesting to preaching without stopping at
home to change, the way he smooths thinning black curls with
the comb in every pair of

pants, his tidy world of black and whites: all hot foods go with
ketchup/all cold foods go with jam, the way he fills his mouth
with every bite and smiles over his glasses at Grandma as he

chews, the way he holds my sticky hand behind the pulpit, his
giant palms—tough and earthy as the burlap sacks of seed I
climb, the Mad Scientist joke books he brings home with the
sugar, so I can follow him around the machine shed trying out my
voice, listening to the high and low of our

laughter echo, the way he refuses to speak his shame over passing
on his damaged chromosomes instead of his faith, the way his
every step reclaims a piece of promised land, his whistles calling
invisible dogs clear across

the field, and after he slides into the care home, trembling, no
longer knowing our names, where we put his money, why he isn't
following her hat through flax or breathing her hair as she

sleeps, the way his prayers still sing.

Daddy insisted that he'd take care
of bringing water to and from
the new washing machine.

So my only job was to give orders,
change clothes in the machine
and hang them out.

Not bad, eh?

Ketchup was used as gravy.

If you had been a bit closer
you could have sent your shirts down too.

And you would not have to trouble
yourself with that kind of stuff.

I shouldn't admit it,
but we finished a bottle.

This Is His Body

Grandpa can't remember my name.

Someone says,
That's not him anymore:
it's just a body.

Yes. My flesh and blood,
embodiment of Christmas hymns
and God.

Grandpa can't remember God anymore.

His blood, a hymn, a firmament
circling.

Grandpa can't remember the days
we sat side by side on
the combine.

Our lungs still sparkling with chaff.

A unique, unquenchable feeling
overwhelms me.

You were beginning to be troubled
by a strange sickness,
"Heimweh," were you not?

I'm troubled
with something very like it, and that is,
"I'm terribly lonesome for you."

Sorry to say, I wasn't able to drop pail or axe
when the mailman came.

I have to keep myself
busy from early till late
to remain master of myself
and my feelings.

I went to tend to my twelve precious
piglets once more and furnished
the stoves with fuel
for the night.

But now I'm off the subject
I started out with completely:

I anew
give you all my love.

Mr. Wiens' sermons were very good.

Threads

Fragile X–associated tremor/ataxia syndrome:
the late-onset degeneration of movement and memory
in some unaffected carriers of Fragile X syndrome.

You lie awake,
needlessly fingering
this patchwork guilt.

Remorse, a code
you live by; distress calls
for someone to blame.

But reason says
the nights
you unbuttoned
her gown

you did not handpick
which chromosomes
to sew—these fragile
threads find their
own bias—

any more than your mother
chose this—the tumbled
thoughts, this late-hour
trembling—
for you.

There is no reason whatsoever
why you should ask me for forgiveness.

Beckoning Hills

Visitors must see the stereoscope for blending into one
two pictures from different points of view

your small-town museum saves

one hundred kinds of barbed wire   a wall of sexy salt shakers
    Dora Ryan's shoe collection circa 1985
mitts sewn from baby seals   a pickled eight-legged pig
    "the tool of unknown use"   the nose
from a cannon projectile sent home
    with Norman Gordon's personal effects

and recovered from turkey gizzards at the poultry plant
this display of rusty nails
white stones
and dice

Preaching to the Choir

The preacher's granddaughter finds the fading
church behind the silos comforting
in its inattentiveness. Storage for things that wait.
From her perch, on spilling bags of grain,
she'll teach crickets to sing, illuminate
each mouse with allegories of sunbeams
on dust, the smell of chaff, the way
the cats she throws off the pallets of seed
always land on their feet.

Dementia, Warm October

These days darkness slumps,
its pants slung low,
hands in its pockets.

I've stopped
covering the tomatoes

but this morning
rose 20 degrees fair,

you return my hello

and we gulp time
like breath.

Even the wasp in my ear
is translated.

This may be the last day the wind
does not hurt my cheeks.

I have struggles which were
unknown to me
in earlier Christian life.

December is certainly giving us
a taste of something better
than November, which was
so dull and misty.

I'll write him
that the Lord's way
is not quite clear to me as yet;

Seldom if ever
did we get a glimpse of the sun.

perhaps the expiration of the war
may be the decisive factor.

But, Abe, should the Lord so lead
our path into his Vineyard:

even in the rough and hard places,

As you write of yourself
I needs must say of myself:

what a comfort to know
"He goes before" (Isaiah 45:2)

I feel incapable.

a road that seems so dark.

Grandpa's Day Timers

1980

Jan. 7	USA embargo causes drop in prices
Jan. 11	Faith for Today
Feb. 27	Seed Growers' meeting
Mar. 20	"The more earnestly I live inwardly, the more simply I'll live without."
April 23	Finished sowing
June 12	Baptismal testimonies

1984

April 28	650 acres in and now snow

1985

Mar. 13	"Prodigal Son"
Mar. 30	Bull sale
June 23	Serve in Justice
July 17	Pick up wallpaper
Aug. 9	Swath Heartland

1987

Mar. 18	Canola Day in Souris
May 28	Ascension Day at Grace
Sept. 10	Cats can
Sept. 21	Cabinet shuffle

1991

Jan. 1	Turning colder
Jan. 18	Visit Pearl Harbor
Jan. 20	Put on the whole armour
Jan. 24	Plane trouble
Feb. 7	Blood pressure
June 27	How are you going to change anybody's mind if your mind is so set.

1997

Jan. 3	Dr. Les DR. LES Dr. Les
Jan. 16	Bath evening, Souris Souris Souris
Jan. 18	heredity cerebral attackia
Jan. 24	Margaret back to Killarney, 1 more week
Feb. 28	I want remote control, remote onrl c
July 17	MAAR GA RETT

For When You Wondered Why I Wasn't There

things grown too loose   (certainty

      clothing) you shed

words (*gravy*

                  granddaughter
) lie tucked like

baby teeth   out of earthly reach
       beneath the pillow

you smile at me and say   *I love you Edith*

I want to tell you   *It's me*

       the one who demanded marshmallow cream
just one more push on the swing

but my aunt Edie was such a beauty at my age (in 1977
       the year you relive in your mind)

and you are so glad

      your little girl is here

Well, Best One,
you haven't returned
that kiss I gave you
in the first letter yet.

The little chicks are coming along very nicely,
we've lost very few up till now.

But I'll steal one tonight.

Daddy and one of the boys
are going to Peters'
to get some coal for the brooder.

I'll only appreciate it so much more
to be with you again

The boys' two main subjects
of conversation are still
skating and trapping muskrats.

and then even in our own little home.

The Minute I Heard You Died

I felt the change in air pressure.
Like when you open a window
and a door slams shut.

After Eights

Every Christmas, I sat
across the kitchen table
as he peeled back my invisible
tape, unfolded the silver wrapping,
pulled open the tiny file box,
its dark sheets of music
crinkling, and slid
a single wafer into his palm.
His wide lips smacked,
his eyes met mine,
as liquid mint
and Old Spice
mingled on his chin.
His deathbed confession:
I never liked them.

For I seemed so concerned about
being alone these days.

When feeding pigs after supper
I have again and again
caught myself
at singing or whistling away

as if I really lived much
above my circumstances.

Funeral Tape

I think about Abe as I prepare for winter

He didn't focus on the other side of us
It may be dark but I want to speak of the future

What Abe would have wanted
God has given

I'd like to leave two verses with you
He made his own ice rink

One is out of Exodus
His time in Evergreen

His first son was
A few words in closing

We're all frail human vessels
I never received a handshake like Abe would give

God has taken
Abe never crumbled

Down the valley one by one
Those who wait on the Lord will be radiant

If we stand under God's hand
It may be dark

To make peace with our past
He bought me joke books

He was tormented
That guy could sing

A few words in closing
We're all frail human vessels

Poor guy had to run behind while I sat on the bike
The road is more pleasant than the Inn

I'd like to leave two verses with you
We forgot our boy at church and pastor brought him home

His time in Evergreen
He said, *You call this an Inn?*

I could talk about Abe as a brother
He prayed as if he meant it

We are going down the valley one by one
The Inn is more pleasant than the road

If you can't see Abe listen for his whistle
I wish I could pull the curtain aside

It may be dark but I want to speak of the future
His time in Evergreen

I think about Abe as I prepare for winter

So you think if you told me
more of what you learned
in your baching career
it may start an argument.

I more resolutely
than ever decided
never to be a bachelor.

Daddy did not ask for leave for you
but rather made another attempt
to get your release.

That has been out of the question
ever since I fell for you, Dearest.

Clouds above Canola

Gardening Advice from the Wife of a Pious Pastor

> *Behold, I send you out as sheep in the midst of wolves;*
> *so be shrewd as serpents and innocent as doves.*
> *—Matthew 10:16*

At her funeral, I daydreamed a black-and-white door flying
wide, a pastor's wife bursting into canola, heavy arms starched
by potatoes, dragging pressed sheets; she falls to her knees in
the dirt, spilling words she could not say to husband, church, six
more itinerant missionaries in upturned hats.

When I was a girl, she sat on the edge of my bed to braid my hair
and whispered, *It's okay to disagree, cross the ocean, feel warm next
to boys, keep a secret, dance inside; we don't talk about love much,
but your Grandpa and I enjoy slipping off our covers.*

When she lay dying, awash in morphine, she pointed one crooked
finger to heaven, and with a blissful smile, yelled, *Your hat looks
silly!* I dreamed we were high as kites, our robes flapping. We
tasted Jell-O, laughed at death.

At her funeral, her neighbour said:

> Margaret walked me through her flower garden, and
> asked, *Which colour do you see first?*

> *White*, I answered.

> Margaret smiled and said, *All you need is a little.*

I came to realize how important it is
that a meal be immediately eaten after
it is prepared.

Now I know you will
in later years remind me of this.

Will I ever get a kick
out of teasing Betty tomorrow
when we go there
to help kill pigs!

Then I'll retort that our home
isn't as cold.

They say the ice
is just perfect at our dugout.

The Autumn of Your Cancer

A north wind has blown you open,
transparent as onion paper

words dangle

your cheeks, frostbitten green tomatoes,
droop from sagging vines

morphine syringe driver chirps a cricket solo

crackling leaves of medical tape
mark your movements
along this path
to dormancy

as if Eurus had exhausted himself
over your skin, the odour of ozone

your lungs sucked shut, layered
in damp asbestos, smoulder

immune to long-term
forecasts, your fingers warm in mine

beyond the window, squirrels scuttle
across fence tops, apples in tight mouths—
you gape, gasp musty breaths,
exhale confessions

guided by brittle bone-memory

stories of shared history
hang between us, perfectly ripened
fruits I cannot catch before they fall, bruised

abundance

I'm not a bit fond of being pitied,
but I took it better than usual,
only because I thought
it's not for long,
soon you'd be here
and all is well.

Scavenger Hunt

In her favourite story

her older sisters hide
behind the chair

pretend to be Russian dolls
so no one will find them

while large men move, squat, grunt,
clean drawers, looking for leavings.

(Their mother tells Makhno's man
        Leave the gun.

She follows him to her bed

        Girls be still.

hopes to make them all
invisible.)

An anarchist sticks their pad of butter
in his back pocket; it melts
and his wide buttocks
begin to leak.

Those girls could have died
laughing.

Between Seed and Harvest

A master of beginnings, great-grandfather,
you turned the Communist closure
of your plow dealership in Neu Samara

(named for the new winged fruit
of ash and maple)
into an excuse to start

the cheese factory you always wanted
the mill where your family never starved
the general store that stood long after

you came to Canada and struggled to become a farmer.
After great-grandma dies and you marry her sister
(their faces indistinguishable in this photograph)

she will try to starve your daughter and leave
your family broken.
There are no fairy-tale endings.

But there are middles.
Your first love
steps off the train in Moscow—

you on leave from the battlefield;
she, running to your arms, crying
Soon we must say goodbye again.

For Your Name's Sake

> *Even though I walk through the darkest valley,*
> *I will fear no evil.*
> —*Psalm* 23:4

from the Greek Margarites:
a pearl

Here is your baby Margaret
who, soon after light imprints
this negative, will spill
into a pail of scalding water.

　　　an irritant
covered with nacre;

Great-grandmother Maria,
you will not give the name
time to dry before pinning it
to another.

after St. Margaret: patron
of expectant mothers;

You will die in childbirth
when your second Margaret
turns two,

　　　legends
tell of her escape from a dragon

and your sister Margaret
will take your life:
husband, house, newborn,

39

and lock your last Margaret
in a closet.

rare, resilient, iridescent

Maria, your faith
in a name can save
at least one.

Dearest Abe,
you weren't exactly lonesome,
were you?

Liebste Margaret,
I liked you putting your head
on my shoulder. It gave me
a feeling that you
relied on me.

It's just too bad
I wasn't so feeble that
you could have given me your arm
for support, isn't it?
We'd be all practised up
by now,

but I think we'll find
time for that yet.

Closure

They circle the casket
of my grandma's father.
Draped in woolen coats,
black armbands.
Squares of white cotton
cover this lip,
that one's eyes.
A woman, her hands
tightly clasped,
scowls at his feet.
Another grips her wrist,
glares at the cut
daffodils that snake
their way across
the displaced earth.
One bows her bare
head, eyes dark,
a pair of white
flowers pinned
above her ear.

Not at this graveside,
my grandma, her flattened
curls. Her first son
lifted from
her halved belly.
He is round and
cold as her father's
buttons.
When she wakes,
she will not be allowed
to say goodbye.

Red speaks of Love, doesn't it?

About tears
that have not yet been shed.

The Night of the Fair

When the rain sneaked up on us

we ran to her condo,
mini-donuts dripping

and sat four generations deep

on her floral sofa.
While our jeans spun dry

we talked about Tsar Nicholas
and Red River spring floods

—laughing over our narrow escape

and my husband's bald chest peeking
out of Grandma's mint-green robe.

*The rain seems to have given us
what we needed today,
a bit of rest.*

Are you sewing, Mom?

my mother asks as
Grandma twines
her fingers through hospital sheets.
I'm planting marigolds,
she answers with a childish
grin. *And tomorrow*
you and I will bake
meat buns for Christmas.

We would sit on the chesterfield with only the
coloured tree-lights shedding their light on us.

Dearest, in years to come,
in some reminiscent hour—

Deep Breathing

The day,
squeezing my husband's thumb
till it throbbed.
How long since we've slept?
The circle of nurses tightens around me

urging
Push, push, more,
push, push, again, more.

Don't you want to see your baby?

Focus on breathing.
slow   in
slow
out
        he's here.

The night,
my hand on Grandma's heavy arm,
feeling for pulse.
Doesn't she look asleep?
Aunts and cousins ring the bed

chanting
You're free, you can go,
we love you, you can go.

Do you see the angels?

Focus on breathing.
nothing   in
nothing
out
        she's gone.

What Little Things Come to Us

In a box of Grandpa's sermons:
a day planner gold-stamped 1987
that Grandma used in 1988,
the seven turned into an eight with the stroke
of a pen.

I marvel at the daily leaps required:
every Thursday crossed out
to become Friday, and after February 29,
she had to think two days ahead.

I now know her windshield
cracked the day Mulroney was re-elected.
She called about her roof the day I turned fifteen.
And the day fifty-plus people came to church,
flax dropped forty cents.

On the page where addresses belong
she wrote:

violets are blue
roses are red
let's go home
enough has been said

There Is the Old Brick House

There is the chocolate-scented doll we found at the Co-op. The yo-yo Grandpa taught me to snap up. The barn cat that finally came close enough to touch.

There is the empty machine shed. The rusted bike. The first time he let go.

There are robin's eggs. Tomato sandwiches on the tailgate.

Grandma's slippers down the hall.

There is the candy jar she slid across the table, the smell of warm play dough on her hands, her oatmeal massaging my cheeks from the inside.

There's the smile in her late-night long-distance hellos. The way she patted her soft hair down as if her life depended on it.

There are clouds above canola—unfinished prayers.

There is the wheat-scented rug. The chimes at three a.m. The afghan she folded around my shoulders.

There is the blistering road to the cemetery, the glossy lake that still fades when I draw near.

FIELDS OF LIGHT AND STONE

Elsa Friesen Falk
(July 20, 1916–April 11, 1998)

Bernhard David Falk
(September 14, 1910–March 2, 2003)

Fields

She was born in a Field of Light.
He was born in a Field of Stone.

They found themselves
in the Strait of the Spirit.

They found each other in the dark.

In the Field of Light
and the Field of Stone

not one stone
remains on another.

In the Strait of the Spirit

he turned over the fields
that once fed buffalo.

She turned over the fields
to their unyielding sons.

The nurses turned out the light.

Shivered into Being

In My First Five Year Diary

no mention of the day
my baby brother walked
into a pool paralyzing me
from the neck down
his blonde hair waving
no record of who dove
for his pale body
the seconds until
he breathed
my first Five Year Diary
does not hold the city boy
who moved in next door
all those afternoons
I hid in the elms
between our fields
to feel his dirt bike
shake the earth
no solar eclipse
no space shuttle disaster
in my first Five Year Diary
went to Oma's house
fills every page

Making Sheep

1.
Then

Yeasty strings web every finger.
She pinches off a balloon of dough
—tests if it will fall.

Now

For the first time, I turn
to the recipe titled "Oma's buns,"
to seek her scent as they rise.

This page in my book is clean.
But my hands know these bubbles,
soft as a belly that's just given birth.

2.
Then

Her swollen knuckles enfold
the apple. Juices dripping on her dress,
she peels away the bruise.

Now

Schaefchen, I whisper—
baby sheep is what she called
these perfect wedges.

      Onto my child's tongue
      they follow, one after
      another.

Unwinding

Saturdays Oma let her hair fall
blue and silver to her waist
and for a moment I could see:

Elsa flit through flax,
a boy chase in circles
to run through her waves,
Elsa brush away braids
before the mirror,
dream of the day
she will let him catch her.

Elsa's girls wash and pin the
locks to her head in a tight roll.
Oma once more.

Oma's Girl

The Sunday sun through chaff-dusted windows
bakes the centre row of white buns—
wisps pinned up tight.
I am wedged between the heavy skirts
that have held this polished pew in its place
since Ezekiel—eyes on every side.
Oma's pale fingers pass a Cert to freeze my tongue,
her hand holds down my bobbing knee—my leotard running.
While the song leader's coattails sway, the chorus rises
under my skin:
the trees of the field clap and *valleys tremble* but
I must be still
and know whose I am.

Bias Binding

> *They sewed fig leaves together and*
> *made coverings for themselves.*
> —*Genesis 3:7*

1.
A rumour generations old, the tale
unfolds like heirloom cloth:

On two brothers' estate lived a sought-after seamstress
and a nameless servant girl.

When the elder brother gave the seamstress carriage rides
through family plots, neighbours nodded.

The younger brother still too rogue
for anything carved in stone.

2.
One night both brothers entered
the servants' quarters.

The younger found the seamstress.
The elder—the servant.

Two girls conceived
daughters in the usual way.

3.
Owing to the younger brother's youth,
the elder was told to marry the seamstress

—chosen for her social standing.
The servant girl was cut loose—

suicide: her second sin.
Strangers cared

for her orphan.

4.
The younger brother grew homeless
while the older brother and the seamstress grew

a farm, a church,
a daughter in tight braids

who listened through plaster
as her parents shivered into being

a son they both could love.

5.
They stitch the story down.
Its shushing of desire.

Come closer. Pull on a thread.
The raw edge
unravels.

In Whispers He's Still the Wanderer

—but was he lost
before that night   he found her

or did his dreams   come loose
   when his brother's family   unfolded
like a letter—   she and her daughter tucked
into its creases?

On nights I toss and yearn   that steady farmer
in her wedding photo   is no longer my ancestor.

In dark times I descend
from the frostbitten wish   flickering

just outside the frame.

All is Bright

Our hair tinseled by tossed-off halos,
we breathe silvery air from the manger
to Oma's front door.

Oma rocks the invisible infant to *Stille Nacht*.
Our distortions stare back from cracked baubles,
lemon candy slices speckling each finger.

Our coats' arms entwine across the sofa.
Another year of faults smothered by gravy,
the centripetal force of snow.

As We Left They Sang

1.
The day they took him
it was muddy.

Children, this time only prayer will help.

The body of our dear father
in the summer room. There was no heat.

The mouth that had so lovingly
sung with us, kissed us.

I went to the garden
until I couldn't cry anymore.

*Mariechen, what you ever were to your father
you will never know.*

2.
October. Black troops stronger
than White chop off limb by limb.

November cannons. Cossacks
to disband the Black.

Christmas night, give
food and lodging for the Red.

We had traded with the Cossacks for some sugar,
but they took it all away.

3.
No rain, our horses taken.
Forced to hitch our cow to the plow.

The second floor once used to store grain:
the remaining kernels.

Things hidden. Our wedding bands.

We lay down
so we wouldn't feel our hunger.

Potatoes the size of hazelnuts.

4.
The caragana trees around our house
in full bloom. After dinner, a light rain.

Our big dog Woljshanck and our little dog Damka
and everything dear to us stayed back.

As we left, they sang, *Jesus, go before us.*
Tears as our train took us away.

Edges

1.

She perches on the edge
of a piano bench
in a Field of Light.

It's 1919 in a Ukraine
before famine and Oma
is singing.

Her lips part so wide
the extravagant sky may
fall in.

2.

I perch on the edge
of a stone flower
bed in a field of dust.

It's 1986 and Oma
is pulling up red geraniums.

Arthritis steadies her,
gives her something painful
to put her finger on.

She moves,
displaces air,
her bones heavy

with skimmed cream,
her voice borrowed
from crows, her arms,
soft petals.

3.
I perch on the edge
of adulthood
in Oma's hospital room.

It's almost Easter 1998 and Oma
is inflated with cancer.

Curled, she imagines peace,
shrinks to fit inside.

Her eyelids fly wide
after her last breath, first
glimpse.

Division

You seem different here, smaller,
though I can barely see your face
over your swollen belly. After eight decades
of deep frying *Rollkuchen*, portioning gravy on potato
mounds, your cancerous abdomen is now eating you.

Your robe splits, and I see your pale hip,
your shaky arm that gropes for the 7UP—
the same arm that reached out
to slap me, pull ribbons—like magic
—from the caverns of chickens,
fell kernels from the cob
(their crumbling towers).

You couldn't have chosen a worse time to take
your leave, your children's children splitting
into nuclear families. You will not meet mine,
but it's okay, you say, you've already prayed for
all of them—and is that sheen
the morphine, or the rheum of angels?

What the Aspens Whispered

Under the Shadow of Your Name

Falk—a falcon

from the Latin—a curved blade,
a pruning hook

a talon, a beak,
the spread of a wing

or the Germanic—
fallow.

Your line
may have been falconers.

Or maybe we descended
from the wild birds—

diving into wide spaces.

He Made Me Promise to Remember Arkadak

> *To have a grandfather is to be spellbound and unsettled,*
> *to be surrounded by languages you can't speak.*
> —Alayna Munce

In Arkadak's crowded market,
vendors yelled what sounds like *yablooka* (apples!)

and *duraki* (you fools!)—Russian words Opa passed me
like forbidden fruit.

He crossed the ocean at nineteen with a new fur coat
and a seven-string guitar that I never saw him play.

Opa slipped brown bills into apron pockets
at the Chicken Chef,

pressed one crisp dollar into my palm every time
he caught me in a skirt.

He peeled apples perfectly with his pocket knife.
I licked the red curls.

He had a smart black hat with a red feather
for Sundays, a grey fur cap with flaps for stamping

through the barn. When Opa took off the hat for dinner,
his hair was a glint of weeping birch bark in the sun.

Opa scraped bedtime stubble across my cheeks.
In the autumn wind, they still burn.

Opa didn't die. He slips
between the apple sellers,

guitar on his back,
younger than I've ever seen him.

When Opa called me *buftya*,
I heard *sweetheart*, my dad heard *pigtail*,

but no Russian I've ever met
knows its meaning

or carries its puff of air inside her
like a seed.

Ancient Script

After I'd brush my teeth, I'd tip
each cheek toward

my parents' goodnight kiss.
And each afternoon

I'd run through the shortcut
to your house

to throw myself
into your arms.

At my high school reunion
beside a barn that once was yours,

I compare success stories,
long to peek inside.

I have no text you wrote,
not a receipt or doodle.

Only your German Bible,
its lines—inscrutable clouds.

Generations

1586: as far back
as the Mennonite database
can take me.

All I find: the surname *Voht*,
a town called *Culm*.

My great-great-great-
great-great-great-
great-great-great-
great-great-grandfather
had a daughter
who had a baby.
And on it goes.

What chases us
down a family tree?
A high forehead?
A voice? A fear?

What drives me to scratch
the earth for these four-letter
kernels?

Voht's daughter named her son
Hans—*God is gracious*,
a promise I can translate.

But I cannot hear
the plea it answered.

Plans to Prosper

Across the street in #6 lived a certain man. He was constantly
coming to borrow tools and flour. He did nothing

as long as father was alive. After father

died he reported us to the authorities *they have ten overcoats: they
are rich.* We gave away what we could. In the middle of the night

prepared to leave everything.

A horse-drawn sleigh to another station—a rented room in a
former dacha of the wealthy—

Canada. Back in #6 the man claimed some of our possessions. But
he got travel fever and held a public auction, which attracted

the attention of police. Internal affairs pocketed the money and
sent him

into exile.

His Hands

Across the bedrail
Opa's heavy hand grips mine
like a doubt.

Here are the bright stumps
my old self, the girl in pigtails,
once wept over.

When I receive
my inheritance, I will open
Opa's German Bible,

and from it, a Last
Supper print will fall,
Jesus' palms up. Scratched
across its back

But woe
to the man by whom
he is betrayed.

I rub Opa's missing fingers.
Dead ends.

A little girl would know how to
kiss them better.

Sunset on Deep Bay

Water the colour of mercury
surrounds me. Only a line of trees
divides the blue above and below.
"What a Wonderful World" carries
from a pinprick of light
across the lake.

Maybe dying is like that. If
you don't turn around
the sand behind you disappears,
the ripples from a distant radio
give the feeling you are moving
closer.

Or maybe
we spend our whole life believing
we could walk on water and death
is the moment we take
our first step.

Souvenir

On my lap, the tarnished
spoons from Opa's travels.
Maps etched into their curves,
tiny ads glued to their handles.

Arizona prickly pear,
Lady Liberty, Bodensee.
From California, a castle
dangles.

All the places
Opa left me for.
The shiny evidence
that he remembered me.

One spoon has lost
its decal. Holding
its mirrored face
close to mine,
I see the last place
he has gone.

After the Funeral, I Pick up My Box

Weighed down by solid oak furniture,
the gravity of grief,

my aunts and uncles divide Opa's home
into boxes.

For the thrift store,
the work clothes worn off the man

who built two farms from the ground
down,

shovelled away snow, soil, and grief
till his heart caved,

went the second mile,

passed me a paint brush, garden hoe,
sticky watermelon kiss.

Others collect his coins.

My inheritance: Opa's crusted boots.

BERNHARD (BEN) D. FALK **After** only three days
in Intensive Care Unit at the **Health** Sciences
Centre, **our** dad, with family at his bedside, went to meet
his Lord and Saviour on Sunday **evening**, **March** 2, 2003,
at the age of 92 years. Dad was born in Steinfeld,
Ukraine, on September 14, 1910, and in 1929 together
with his family, immigrated to Canada and settled
in the Niverville area. Dad met Elsie Friesen and
on September 10, 1938, the **two became one in Holy**
Matrimony and shared **almost** 60 years together.
They farmed near Niverville with **their** four **oldest** sons
until their retirement in 1986. In April of 1998, his be**loved**
wife Elsie passed away. A celebration of Dad's
life will be held on Friday, March 7, 2:00 p.m. at
the Niverville 4th Avenue Bible Church with viewing
at Loewen Funeral Chapel in Steinbach on Thursday,
March 6, 7:00 to 8:00 p.m. with **meditation to follow**
at 8:00 p.m. Interment will follow in the Niverville
Cemetery. Should friends so **desire**, donations may be
made in Dad's **memory** to Gospel Outreach Ministry
to Ukraine (a charity that Dad faithfully supported),
available at the church.

Arrangements entrusted to Loewen Funeral Chapel.
Send **flowers** to the family

As published in the Winnipeg Free **Press on** *March 05, 2003*

The First Trees

Aspens are the first trees
to recover, to spread after all life
has been cut down or burned away,
their shared roots resting below the heat
of greed and betrayal, their sibilant leaves turning
gold in unison—like the veering of swallows.
The weightiest living thing on earth
is an aspen stand, 47,000 trunks strong.
Tens of thousands of years before flight, Pando
began like all seeds—
with an idea, and the soil caught wind of it.
Lighter than oak or regret, aspen crates are perfect
for carrying the books our ancestors
have yet to write.

Love Letters, 1944–45
Flowing throughout the section entitled "In Some Reminiscent
Hour," these poems are excerpts of correspondence between the
author's grandparents Abram Froese (on the left margins) and
Margaret Dueck (on the right). Most of these letters were written
while Abram was a conscientious objector in Ontario during the
Second World War and Margaret was living with her father and
brothers in Boissevain, Manitoba, on the farm she and Abram
would later inherit. *Heimweh* is German for "homesickness."

Resurrection
"God's house has many rooms" is from John 14:2, one of Abram
Froese's favourite Scripture passages.

Beckoning Hills
Beckoning Hills is a museum in Boissevain, Manitoba.

Grandpa's Day Timers
A found poem of handwritten notes from Abram Froese's
calendars. He attributed the quote to Ernest Hemingway.

Funeral Tape
This poem is made of phrases guests shared at the mic at Abram
Froese's funeral in Boissevain, Manitoba, October 25, 1997, based
on the audiotape recording. "The road is...better than the inn" is a
quote from *Don Quixote de la Mancha* by Miguel de Cervantes.

Scavenger Hunt
This poem is loosely based on the description of events that took
place in Pleshanov, Neu Samara, Russia, in the unpublished
memoir of Margaret Dueck Froese's sister Katie Dueck Martens,
transcribed by Margaret, typed by Margaret's daughter-in-
law Elaine Edie Froese in December 1996. Nestor Makhno
commanded an independent army of anarchists in South Russia
following the Revolution of 1917.

Between Seed and Harvest
Margaret Froese's father Gerhard Dueck served with the Red
Cross during the First World War, carrying wounded Russian
soldiers off the battlefield and taking them by train to Moscow.

Closure
The funeral scene in "Closure" is based on a photograph of
Margaret Froese's father Gerhard Dueck's funeral in 1952.

Fields
"Field of Light" is a translation of Lichtfelde and "Field of Stone"
of Steinfeld, two villages in the Molotschna Mennonite colony in
Ukraine. "Strait of the Spirit" is a translation of Manitoba, which
is believed to have come from Cree or Ojibwe.

Making Sheep
Schaefchen means "little sheep," Elsa Falk's term for apple slices.

Oma's Girl
"The trees of the field clap" is based on Isaiah 55:12.

Bias Binding and *In Whispers He's Still the Wanderer*
These two poems are based on unconfirmed verbal reports passed
down the generations from the "younger brother/wanderer."
While there is no written evidence to support these stories'
veracity, they are included because of their effect on the author's
imagination.

As We Left They Sang
This found poem comes from lines in the unpublished memoir of
Elsa Falk's mother Maria Janzen Friesen, translated from German
into English by Elsa and Elsa's daughter Viola Toews. Events
described in the poem took place in Ukraine from 1910 to 1924.

He Made Me Promise to Remember Arkadak
The epigraph is from *When I Was Young and In My Prime*, Alayna
Munce, Nightwood Editions, 2005, www.nightwoodeditions.com.

Plans to Prosper
This poem is based on Peter Letkemann's notes from his July 16,
2001, interview with Bernhard David Falk in Niverville, Manitoba.
Village #6 was in Arkadak, Russia, where Bernhard spent most of
his youth, immigrating to Canada in 1929. Letkemann's research
is published in *A Book of Remembrance: Mennonites in Arkadak
and Zentral, 1908–1941*, Old Oak Publishing, 2016.

His Hands
"Woe to the man by whom he is betrayed" is a reference to Luke
22:22.

A note on biblical passages
John 12:24, Psalm 23:4, and Genesis 3:7 are from the New
International Version. Matthew 10:16 is from the New American
Standard Bible. 1 Kings 19:11–12 is from the Contemporary
English Version.

ACKNOWLEDGEMENTS

The author acknowledges that the fields her maternal great-grandparents and grandparents cultivated near Boissevain, Manitoba, are in Treaty 2 territory, the traditional territory of Anishinaabeg, Cree, Oji-Cree, Assiniboine, Dakota, Dene, and Métis. The land her paternal grandparents and parents farmed near Niverville, Manitoba, and where she spent her childhood, is in Treaty 1 territory, the original lands of Anishinaabeg, Cree, Oji-Cree, Dakota, and Dene peoples, and homeland of the Métis Nation.

Thank you to family members who shared recollections and historical documents. While this book tries to accurately represent the past, some of *Fields of Light and Stone* may be attributed to the ways memory is imperfect and the author's imagination shapes the poems.

The writer is grateful to Conrad Stoesz and Peter Letkemann for their help with historical and genealogical research, to Peter Midgley, Joanne Epp, and Jennifer Still for their feedback on this volume, and to the Manitoba Arts Council and Winnipeg Arts Council for financial support during its creation.

Many thanks to the staff at University of Alberta Press for bringing this book to life, to Miriam Rudolph for the beautiful cover image, and to Alice Major for her thoughtful edits.

Thank you the editors of the following publications in which versions of poems in this collection have previously appeared:

Canadian Literature: "Sunset on Deep Bay"

Contemporary Verse 2: "He Made Me Promise to Remember Arkadak"

Grain: an excerpt from "Love Letters, 1944–1945"

Journal of Mennonite Writing: "Grandpa's Day Timers," "As We Left They Sang," and "Plans to Prosper"

Leafpress.ca Monday's Poem and Winnipeg International Writers Festival *Say the Word* project: "Everything There Is to Say"

Lemon Hound: "Funeral Tape"

Onesentencepoems.com: "For When You Wondered Why I Wasn't There"

Rhubarb: "Tokens of Mercy," "Gardening Advice from the Wife of a Pious Pastor," "Scavenger Hunt," "Division," "Everything There Is to Say," and "After the Funeral, I Pick up My Box"

Roads of Stone (Alfred Gustav Press, 2015): "The Autumn of Your Cancer"

Beautiful Women: An Anthology (Lipstick Press, 2013): "Unwinding"

The Society: "Making Sheep"

Whale Road Review: "Are you sewing, Mom?"